EYEWITNESS TO HISTORY

ABIGAIL

in her own words

Gareth Stevens
Publishing

By Blair Belton

Please visit our website, www.garethstevens.com. For a free color catalog of all our high-quality books, call toll free 1-800-542-2595 or fax 1-877-542-2596.

Library of Congress Cataloging-in-Publication Data

Belton, Blair.
Abigail Adams in her own words / by Blair Belton.
  p. cm. — (Eyewitness to History)
Includes index.
ISBN 978-1-4339-9871-3 (pbk.)
ISBN 978-1-4824-3316-6 (6-pack)
ISBN 978-1-4339-9870-6 (library binding)
1. Adams, Abigail, — 1744-1818 — Juvenile literature. 2. Presidents' spouses — United States — Biography — Juvenile literature. I. Title.
E322.1.A38 B45 2014
973.4—dc23

First Edition

Published in 2014 by
Gareth Stevens Publishing
111 East 14th Street, Suite 349
New York, NY 10003

Designer: Katelyn E. Reynolds
Editor: Therese Shea

Photo credits: Cover, pp. 1, 7 (Abigail) Mansell/Time & Life Pictures/Getty Images; cover, p. 1 (background illustration) Kean Collection/Getty Images; cover, p. 1 (logo quill icon) Seamartini Graphics Media/Shutterstock.com; cover, p. 1 (logo stamp) YasnaTen/Shutterstock.com; cover, p. 1 (color grunge frame) DmitryPrudnichenko/Shutterstock.com; cover, pp. 1–32 (paper background) Nella/Shutterstock.com; cover, pp. 1–32 (decorative elements) Ozerina Anna/Shutterstock.com; pp. 1–32 (wood texture) Reinhold Leitner/Shutterstock.com; pp. 1–32 (open book background) Elena Schweitzer/Shutterstock.com; pp. 1–32 (bookmark) Robert Adrian Hillman/Shutterstock.com; p. 5 Benjamin Blythe/Wikipedia.com; p. 7 (John) Kean Collection/Getty Images; p. 9 Arthur C. Haskell for the Historic American Buildings Society/Wikipedia.com; pp. 10–11, 26 Mansell/Time & Life Pictures/Getty Images; p. 13 Jogn Parrot/Stocktrek Images/Getty Images; p. 15 (signature) Slashme/Wikipedia.com; pp. 15 (image), 24–25, 27 MPI/Getty Images; p. 17 SuperStock/Getty Images; pp. 18–19 PhotoQuest/Getty Images; p. 20 Stock Montage/Getty Images; p. 23 Courtesy the private collection of Roy Winkelman/Educational Technology Clearinghouse/University of South Florida.

Printed in the United States of America

CPSIA compliance information: Batch #CW14GS: For further information contact Gareth Stevens, New York, New York at 1-800-542-2595.

CONTENTS

*Words in the glossary appear in **bold** type the first time they are used in the text.*

WHO WAS
Abigail Adams?

MORE TO KNOW

Having a reliable way to communicate by mail was so important that the temporary US government created a postal service with Benjamin Franklin as its head in 1775. There was a US post office before there was a permanent government!

Abigail Smith was born in Massachusetts in 1744 and married John Adams in 1764. John was one of the Founding Fathers of the United States. He served in US government, as an ambassador in Europe, and then as the second president of the United States. Abigail was also the mother of John Quincy Adams, who became the sixth president.

Abigail wrote many letters to her husband, family, and friends. Through these letters we can see what she thought of historic events and famous people. Some of her writing appears incorrect by today's rules, since rules for spelling, capitalization, and punctuation were different at that time. Also, Abigail didn't go to school and, with some help from her parents, mostly taught herself by reading books and writing to others.

This portrait of Abigail Adams was painted shortly after she married John Adams.

MAIL PROBLEMS

In colonial times, letters were often carried by the first person traveling in the right direction. Abigail wrote about the difficulties of sending letters after having missed two carriers: *"This Letter has been very unlucky haveing mist [missed] two Opportunities."* Writing paper was sometimes scarce: *"I must beg the favour of you to send me . . . paper."* Letters could also be **intercepted** by enemies: *"He mentions certain intercepted Letters which he says have made much Noise in England."*

A TIME OF *Disease*

FIGHTING DISEASE WITH DISEASE

A few months before Abigail and John married, he was inoculated against **smallpox**. This meant he received a weak dose of smallpox so that his body would be able to fight the disease in the future. However, he could infect others. Putting an infected person's letters in smoke was believed to kill the disease. Abigail wrote in April 1764: *"I hope you smoke your Letters well, before you deliver them."* John wrote back there was *"real Danger, in Writing."*

Deadly diseases were common in Abigail's lifetime, and illnesses were a common topic in her letters. The term "distemper" was used for many diseases. In September 1775, there was an **epidemic** of **dysentery**, during which Abigail's mother died. Abigail wrote, *"Tis a dreadful time . . . Sickness and death are in almost every family. I have no more shocking and terible Idea of any Distemper except the Plague than this."*

Abigail also wrote about an illness she called throat distemper on April 5, 1776: *"Many grown persons are now sick with it, . . . It rages much in other Towns. The*

Mumps too are very frequent." In the same letter, she said, "*I am fearfull of the small pox, or I should have been in [Boston] before this time.*"

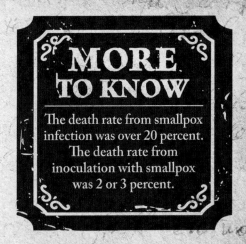

| WILLIAM SMITH | ELIZABETH QUINCY | | JOHN ADAMS | SUSANNA BOYLSTON |

ABIGAIL SMITH ADAMS

JOHN ADAMS

| ABIGAIL (NABBY) (1765) | SUSANNA (1768) | THOMAS BOYLSTON (1772) |

| JOHN QUINCY (1767) | CHARLES (1770) |

This is the family tree of Abigail and John Adams. Abigail and John's daughter Susanna died at the age of 2.

THE BEGINNINGS
of Revolution

In 1774, the British controlled Boston, but not the countryside around it. When the British tried to capture a supply of the colonists' gunpowder, the colonists hid their gunpowder further from Boston. Abigail wrote on September 14, 1774: *"There pass[ed] by here about 200 Men, preceeded by a horse cart, and marched down to the powder house from whence they took the powder and carried [it] into the other **parish**."*

The First Continental Congress, a meeting of representatives from all colonies except for Georgia, formed in response to some harsh British laws, especially against Massachusetts. Abigail saw the Continental Congress as John's chance to be a leader. Abigail wrote to John in August 1774: *"I long impatiently to have you upon the Stage of action."*

On September 1, 1774, British troops removed the gunpowder stored at the Old Powder House in the village of Somerville, Massachusetts. Abigail witnessed her village moving their gunpowder to a new hiding place.

WARTIME HARDSHIPS

A British **blockade** of Boston beginning in 1774 made life much harder on the colonists. The prices of everyday items such as pins for sewing and paper for letter writing rose. Sometimes items just weren't available. Abigail wrote on June 16, 1775: *"The cry for pins is so great that what we used to Buy for 7.6 are now 20 Shillings and not to be had for that."* (Shillings were British units of money that the colonies used.)

After the Battles of Lexington and Concord in April 1775, British troops were trapped in Boston with American colonial forces closing in. The colonists dug trenches on high ground across the river from Boston. Upon seeing this, the British attacked the Americans there, and the conflict became known as the Battle of Bunker Hill. The British also set fire to the village of Charlestown.

Abigail wrote on June 18, 1775: *"Charlstown is laid in ashes. The Battle began upon our*

FALLEN FRIEND

Dr. Joseph Warren was the president of the Massachusetts Provincial Congress. Abigail wrote about his part in the Battle of Bunker Hill: *"Our dear Friend Dr. Warren is no more but fell gloriously fighting for his Country."* Warren was killed while encouraging the American colonists to fight on even as the British attacked: *"He has distinguished himself in every engagement, by his courage and fortitude, by animating the Soldiers and leading them on by his own example."*

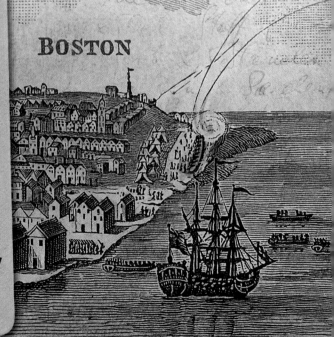

BOSTON

*intrenchments [**entrenchments**] upon Bunkers Hill, a Saturday morning about 3 o'clock and has not ceased yet."* The battle was so loud that it could be heard where Abigail lived. *"How [many have] fallen we know not—the constant roar of the cannon is so [distressing] that we can not Eat, Drink or Sleep."*

MORE TO KNOW

John Quincy Adams remembered watching the Battle of Bunker Hill from a hill near his family farm when he was 7.

CHARLES TOWN

ABIGAIL AND *the Declaration of Independence*

In 1776, the Second Continental Congress in Philadelphia, Pennsylvania, discussed whether to declare independence from England. They adopted the Declaration of Independence on July 4, 1776.

Abigail learned about the Declaration on July 13 in a letter from John. She wrote back to him that she was very pleased *"by the prospect of the future happiness and glory of our Country; nor am I a little Gratified when I reflect that a person so nearly connected with me has had the Honour of being a principal actor, in laying a foundation for its future Greatness."* She knew that the Declaration of Independence was important for the country and that her husband had a major part in writing it.

FAMILY LIFE GOES ON

Even while the United States was forming, Abigail was focused on taking care of her family. She took her children to Boston on July 12, 1776: *"I yesterday arrived and was with all 4 of our Little ones innoculated for the small pox."* John Quincy, Thomas, and Abigail had mild cases. Nabby had a very severe case, while Charles required more than one inoculation. Abigail didn't leave Boston until September 2.

John Adams believed that July 2, the day the Declaration of Independence was approved, would be the national holiday, not July 4. He wrote, *"The Second Day of July 1776 . . . will be celebrated, by succeeding Generations, as the great anniversary Festival."*

This painting shows (from left to right) Benjamin Franklin, John Adams, and Thomas Jefferson drafting the Declaration of Independence.

STAYING
in Touch

MORE TO KNOW

Abigail and John were separated for years when he went to Europe in 1778. She sailed to Europe to be with him in 1784.

Abigail and John spent many years apart because of his work. She missed him, and so did the Adams children. Once, when the children were small, Abigail wrote to John about the scene at home when a packet of his letters arrived:

It would have grieved you if you had seen your youngest Son stand by his Mamma and when she deliverd out to the others their Letters, he inquired for one, but none appearing he stood in silent grief with the Tears running down his face, nor could he be pacified till I gave him one of mine. Pappa does not Love him he says so well as he does Brothers, and many comparisons were made to see whose Letters were the longest.

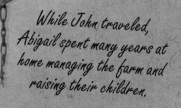

While John traveled, Abigail spent many years at home managing the farm and raising their children.

LOST LETTERS

The only communications between Abigail and John when they were apart were letters that were often delayed or lost. In 1778, John—whom Abigail called her *"Dearest Friend"*—made the dangerous voyage to Paris across the Atlantic Ocean. Abigail didn't hear from him for 4 months. She finally read in a newspaper about his arrival at the Paris home of Benjamin Franklin: *"Under the Paris News there is mention made of my Dearest Friends arrival at the abode of the **venerable** Dr. Frankling."*

Abigail's actual signature:

Abigail Adams

ABIGAIL'S *Beliefs*

THE CONSTITUTIONAL CONVENTION

In 1787, Abigail wrote about the **Constitutional Convention** as they constructed a new constitution. She feared that some would use their power to write laws to become rich and join in groups to prevent agreement. The states needed a strong government to stay together and jointly oppose foreign enemies. *"I wish most sincerely that the meeting of our Convention . . . may reform abuses, Reconcile parties, give energy to Government & stability to the States."*

Before the Declaration of Independence, there was much discussion about what kind of government the new country should adopt. Abigail had concerns about this and wrote on November 27, 1775:

*I am more and more convinced . . . that power whether **vested** in many or a few is ever grasping . . . The great fish swallow up the small, . . . if we seperate from Brittain, what Code of Laws will be established. How shall we be governd so as to retain our Liberties?*

Abigail feared that any new government would become too powerful, whether it was a single king or many members in a legislature.

Those in control would *swallow up* the rights and freedoms of ordinary citizens. She wondered what laws could keep this from happening.

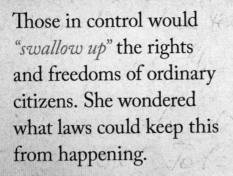

On September 17, 1787, the delegates to the Constitutional Convention signed the new US Constitution. This artist shows people celebrating, including George Washington (in black).

MORE TO KNOW

Abigail was sometimes frustrated by how people behaved after the new nation was established. In 1793, she wrote, *"The Halcion [Halcyon] days of America are past I fully believe."* "Halcyon days" means a time of peace and happiness.

Women in colonial times didn't have the right to vote, and most couldn't own property.

Women were treated by the law much like children. Before the Declaration of Independence was written, Abigail wrote to her husband in Philadelphia about including rights for women in the new country: *"In the new Code of Laws . . . I desire you would Remember the*

Ladies, and be more generous and favourable to them than your ancestors."

Abigail was one of the first to speak out for women's rights. Her letters are proof that people expressed the desire for gender equality from the beginning of the United States. However, the Declaration of Independence didn't mention any rights for women.

American women didn't receive the right to vote until 1920.

EDUCATION FOR WOMEN

Most girls didn't go to school when Abigail was growing up. She taught herself about the world by reading books and writing letters to knowledgeable people. She wrote to her husband about the need to educate women: *"If we mean to have Heroes, Statesmen and Philosophers, we should have learned women."* She wrote this knowing that the idea wasn't popular: *"The world perhaps would laugh at me, and accuse me of vanity."*

VOTE VOTE VOTE VOTE

EDUCATION FOR EVERYONE

In 1797, Abigail helped a freed black man attend a local school in Massachusetts. A neighbor complained to her. Abigail wrote to John that the neighbor was *"attacking the principle of Liberty and equality upon the only Ground upon which it ought to be supported, an equality of Rights. The Boy is a Freeman as much as any of the young Men, and merely because his Face is Black, is he to be denied instruction?"*

In September 1774, British officials in Boston discussed freeing slaves if they took up arms against the colonists. Abigail wrote, *"I wish most sincerely there was not a Slave in the province. It allways appeard a most **iniquitious** Scheme to me—fight ourselfs for what we are daily robbing and plundering from those who have as good a right to freedom as we have."*

In March 1776, Abigail had doubts that slave owners could fight for freedom when they wouldn't allow their slaves to be free. She wrote to her husband, *"I have sometimes been ready to think that the passion for Liberty cannot be Eaquelly Strong in the Breasts of those who have been accustomed to deprive their fellow Creatures of theirs."*

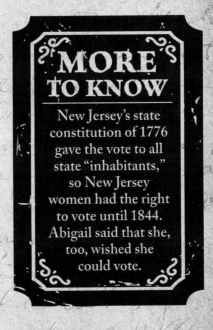

MORE TO KNOW

New Jersey's state constitution of 1776 gave the vote to all state "inhabitants," so New Jersey women had the right to vote until 1844. Abigail said that she, too, wished she could vote.

This portrait of Abigail Adams dates back to 1790.

NORTH AND
South Divisions

PREDICTING THE CIVIL WAR

There would be more compromises between North and South in the years to come. Abigail wrote to her sister Mary in 1792: *"I firmly believe if I live Ten Years longer, I shall see a devision of the Southern & Northern States."* Abigail was correct in predicting the division between North and South, but not correct in the date. That came with the start of the American Civil War (1861–1865).

From the first meeting of the Continental Congress, there were disagreements between the northern, mostly free, states and the southern slave-owning states. A major compromise to keep the country together came in 1790. A new national capital was planned in Washington, DC, closer to southern states. In return, southern states agreed to a new plan to pay off the debts of the American Revolution.

Every issue seemed to bring about conflict between North and South. Abigail wrote to John in 1794: *"The North and South appear to be arranged very **formidably** against each other on politicks."* Abigail commented to her sister Elizabeth in 1798, *"I hope we may be held together, but I know not* how long, for oil and water are not more contrary in their natures, than North and South."

MORE TO KNOW

Abigail's son John Quincy Adams worked to end slavery when he was a congressman from 1830 to 1848.

In Abigail's lifetime, the nation was divided between states that allowed slavery and those that didn't.

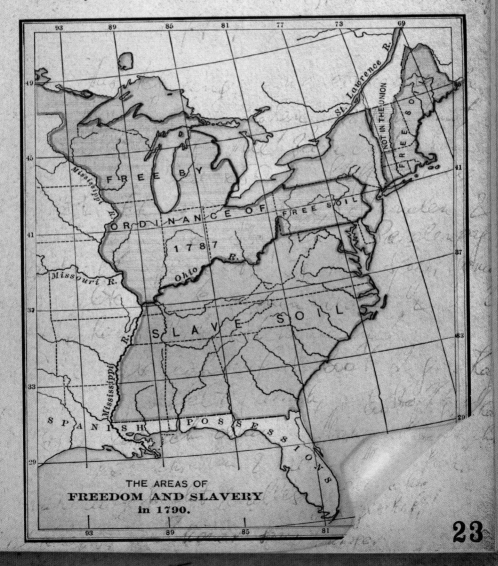

THE AREAS OF
FREEDOM AND SLAVERY
in 1790.

MEETING

Famous People

Abigail met George Washington for the first time in July 1775, when he came to Boston to take command of the Americans' Continental army. John had told Abigail how he admired Washington. Abigail wrote:

> *I was struck with General Washington. You had prepared me to entertain a favorable opinion of him, but I thought the one half was not told me.* **Dignity** *with ease, and* **complacency***, the Gentleman and Soldier look agreably blended in him. Modesty marks every line and feture [feature] of his face.*

MORE TO KNOW

Abigail and John were friends with Thomas Jefferson for many years. Though John and Thomas became opponents in politics, they set aside their differences in later years.

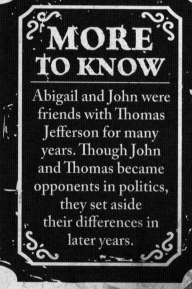

Abigail thought that John had understated just how dignified, how fine a soldier, and how modest a leader George Washington was. The future US president told Abigail that he had *"regard,"* or respect, for John as well.

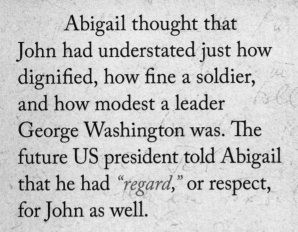

George Washington traveled to Boston in July 1775 to take command of the Continental army.

PAUL REVERE

Paul Revere is famous for warning the countryside when the British troops were marching to Lexington and Concord in 1775. When the Continental Congress was meeting in Philadelphia, Paul Revere traveled between Boston and Philadelphia as a trusted messenger. He also carried mail for Abigail Adams. Abigail mentions him in a letter to her husband who was then in Philadelphia: *"I hope to hear from you by the return of the bearer of this and by Revere."*

In 1779, John Adams went to France to begin to work on a peace treaty with England. In 1784, Abigail moved to Paris to be with him. While in Europe, Abigail met many people, including John Paul Jones, the American naval hero. Abigail had expected a large, rugged man like an ancient Roman soldier. She was surprised by how small and gentle he appeared. She wrote:

*From the **intrepid** Character he justly Supported in the American Navy, I expected to have seen a Rough Stout warlike Roman. Instead of that I should sooner think of wrapping him up in a cotton wool and putting him in my pocket than sending him to contend with cannon-balls.*

JOHN PAUL JONES

John Paul Jones sailed an American warship to Europe in 1777 to bring the war to the British homeland. He prepared a large warship while in France and named it the *Bonhomme Richard*. In 1779, he led the *Bonhomme Richard* into battle against the better-armed British ship *Serapis*. The *Bonhomme Richard* was pounded by cannon fire and seriously damaged. Jones shouted, *"I have not yet begun to fight!"* and soon captured the *Serapis*.

However, Abigail admitted that *"Under all this appearance of softness he is Bold enterprising and active."*

The battle between the Bonhomme Richard and the Serapis made John Paul Jones famous.

MORE TO KNOW

Abigail knew how important a navy was to the Americans in the war for independence. She wrote in May 1781, *"We wish for a Naval force superiour to what we have yet had."*

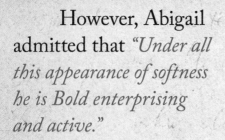

A PLACE
in History

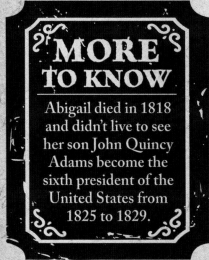

MORE TO KNOW

Abigail died in 1818 and didn't live to see her son John Quincy Adams become the sixth president of the United States from 1825 to 1829.

Abigail Adams experienced many historic events: the blockade of Boston, the Battles of Lexington and Concord, and the Battle of Bunker Hill. Through her husband, she knew about the writing of the Declaration of Independence, the peace treaty with England, and the writing of the US Constitution. Abigail met many of the people we read about in history books, and she became one as the First Lady of the United States.

Throughout all this, Abigail raised four children, managed a farm, survived repeated epidemics, and made the voyage to Europe. Abigail has long been admired for her wit, opinions, and insights. Her many letters to her husband, family, and friends are invaluable to those who wish to learn what life was really like in those times.

TIMELINE
THE LIFE OF ABIGAIL ADAMS

Abigail is born — **1744**

1764 — Abigail and John marry

Abigail (Nabby) is born — **1765**

1767 — John Quincy is born

Susanna is born — **1768**

1770 — Charles is born

Thomas Boylston is born — **1772**

1774 — British blockade of Boston begins

Battles of Lexington and Concord fought

1774 — First Continental Congress forms

Battle of Bunker Hill fought — **1775**

1783 — Peace treaty ending the American Revolution

Abigail joins John in Paris — **1784**

1789 — John elected vice president

John elected president — **1796**

1797 — Abigail becomes First Lady

Abigail moves into the White House — **1800**

1818 — Abigail dies

Abigail wrote about the problems that faced the governing of a new United States. She had many ideas that were ahead of her time, such as racial equality and equal rights for women. All were based on her belief in treating others the way she would want to be treated. She called it the *"principle of doing to others, as we would have others do to us."*

GLOSSARY

blockade: the blocking of harbors to keep people and supplies from coming and going

complacency: self-satisfaction

Constitutional Convention: a meeting that took place in 1787 to address problems in the original US constitution, the Articles of Confederation

dignity: a sense of pride and self-respect

dysentery: a disease of the digestive system

entrenchment: a long hole dug in the ground as a means of defense

epidemic: an outbreak of disease

formidably: with great strength, size, or ability

iniquitous: wicked or acting with great injustice

intercept: to prevent people or objects from reaching their destinations

intrepid: fearless

parish: a community

smallpox: an illness caused by a microorganism called a virus

venerable: worthy of respect

vest: to give power to

FOR MORE
Information

Books

Sawyer, Kem Knapp. *Abigail Adams*. New York, NY: DK Publishing, 2009.

Somervill, Barbara A. *Abigail Adams: Courageous Patriot and First Lady*. Minneapolis, MN: Compass Point Books, 2006.

Wheeler, Jill C. *Abigail Adams*. Edina, MN: ABDO, 2010.

Websites

Abigail Adams
www.biography.com/people/abigail-adams-9175670?page=1
Read a short biography of Abigail Adams and watch videos about her life.

Adams Family Papers
www.masshist.org/digitaladams/aea/index.html
This site allows you to see the original letters of John and Abigail Adams.

John & Abigail Adams
www.pbs.org/wgbh/amex/adams/peopleevents/index.html
This PBS site has many links to more information about the Adams family.

INDEX